Macclesfield Memories

an old picture postcard album

by

Gordon Campbell

Cheshire
Libraries

Dedicated to my wife Gi, who has shown remarkable patience with my
"load of grotty postcards" lying around and who has devoted the whole
of our married life to bringing up our daughter and two sons, as well
as looking after me, which is no easy task.

Cheshire Libraries and Museums
91, Hoole Road,
Chester CH2 3NG

First published 1985

ISNB   0   904532 16 X

Introduction

This is a book with a difference. It is composed entirely of old postcards of the Macclesfield area and is compiled from my own collection which has been built up over the years from places as far afield as Australia, South Africa, Canada, the Channel Isles and several European countries.

Postcard collecting (Deltiology) is now the second most popular collecting hobby after Stamps (Philately), and is well ahead of Cigarette Cards (Cartophily) and the acquisition of other memorabilia.

Picture postcards began around 1880, the earliest cards, Vignettes, having undivided backs on which one was only allowed to write the name and address — any message had to be scribbled on the front. The divided backs which we know today only appeared early in the present century. The Germans were the pioneers of chromolithography in colouring postcards, which meant that British photographers had to send all their slides by sea to Germany for processing and return. Such cards can often be identified by the words 'printed in Bavaria, Saxony' etc. on the reverse, but sometimes this clue to origin was inserted in the stamp corner, making it difficult to ascertain where a card was produced if it had been posted.

Not surprisingly this trade came to an end with the outbreak of hostilities in 1914!

In Victorian and Edwardian times it cost a halfpenny to send a postcard to someone in this country but in 1918 the rate was doubled to one penny and, for a time, demand fell away. There were, however, many different postcard publishers, some still active today. They included Tuck, Valentine, Judge, Frith, Bamforth, Salmon, Photochrom, Dennis, Hartmann, Cynicus, Boots, W.H. Smith and many others. Themes used by the postcard manufacturers were rich and varied but, in general, topographicals were most popular, especially real photo.

Macclesfield had a number of photographers whose work appeared in postcard format. The best known, perhaps, were Bullock and Sons who began in the middle of the last century in Buckley Terrace, had studios at 2, Hibel Road and later opened premises in Congleton and Stockport. Other local photographers included: Leech's (subsequently taken over by Robert Hughes); F. Buckley of 51, Old Park Lane; R. White at 3, Park Street; Bay State Photo Company, 24, Daybrook Street and J. Albinson, operating from 28, Roe Street.

I first became acquainted with Macclesfield when my family moved here from our native Tyneside in 1954 and it did not take long for my interest in postcard collecting to extend to items from my newly-adopted home town.

Macclesfield is an old Mill town, at one time heavily dependent on the silk industry, which became a Borough in 1261 and was granted a Royal Charter seven hundred years later in 1961. It was my work in the textile business which brought me to the "Home of Silk", as Macclesfield is often known. However, it has also been known to many as "Treacle Town". The story goes that one day a horse and cart, laden with barrels of treacle, was making its way down the hill in Mill Street when one of the barrels fell off. The barrel smashed open on the pavement and the ladies living nearby dashed out with their ladles and bowls to scoop it up. It was also said that rations of treacle were distributed to the local silk workers, although these claims have never been substantiated!

The population of Macclesfield remained fairly static for many years. In 1891 it numbered 36,009, in 1960 it was 36,830 and only when ICI Pharmaceuticals relocated their headquarters in Hurdsfield and Alderley Edge, and were followed by others such as Ciba-Geigy, did the population figure start to climb until in the mid-1980's it exceeded 40,000 in the town itself.

When the Borough received its Royal Charter the second lady Mayor, Councillor Mrs. Lily Davenport, was in office, the first having been Mrs. Amy Marian White ten years earlier. Mrs. Davenport was to serve as Mayor on three subsequent occasions; 1970, 1971 and 1973 until Local Government Reorganisation took place in April 1974 bringing into existence a new and larger Borough which covers an area of over 200 square miles and has a total population of almost 150,000.

I hope that all will enjoy reading this book and that looking at these old postcards will bring back memories for the older generation, as well as stimulating in the younger generation an interest in "the way we were" in Macclesfield!

Gordon Campbell
Macclesfield 1985.

1. Coat of Arms *Nec Virtus Nec Copia Desunt*: "Neither courage nor plenty are lacking," the motto and coat of arms of Macclesfield Borough until Local Government Reorganisation in April 1974. 'Courage' was symbolised by the Macclesfield Lion and 'plenty' by the Cheshire Wheatsheaf. Since Reorganisation a new motto has been adopted, *Memores Boni Consilli*: "Mindful of our worthy cause."

2. Multiple view, twelve miniature pictures of Macclesfield and district on a card produced by F. Hartmann and posted to Congleton in April 1906.

3. Macclesfield Town Hall was first built in the 1820's with the entrance at the side by the Church. Between 1869 and 1871 another entrance with more porticos was added at the front of the building. The card illustrated is an unusual 'Alumino' type, produced pre-1914 in the Palatine series.

4. Market Place in the early 1920's showing Union Gateway and Unicorn Gateway. These entries beside the Town Hall were referred to as 'gennels' by some Maxonians and 'ginnels' by others. All that remain now are the signs. At the back of this area were several public houses, now demolished, but on the right can be seen the 'Bull's Head'. On the left are the premises of Salter and Salter, well-known scale manufacturers but no longer operating in the town.

5. The corner of **Market Place** showing Leach's Chemists and the London Tailoring Company. On the right is the entrance to Stanley Street, where Redman's have been replaced by Ratner's Jewellers, and Hadfield's Chemists by the Nationwide Building Society.

6. Brunswick Hill, at the rear of the new Police Station.

7. Chestergate, from a pre-1914 post-card printed in Saxony. On the left is Parr's Penny Bank, now the National Westminster Bank, with Boots Cash Chemists on the right. In those days there were also doctors' and dentists' surgeries in this main shopping thoroughfare.

8. Reputed to be Macclesfield's oldest pub, although long demolished, this is the **"Sun Inn"** at the turn of the century. The card was produced by Brunt and Co., printers in Mill Street.

9. A long vista of shops, many with sunblinds erected, stretching down **Chestergate** towards the Town Hall about 1904. An elderly lady known to the author believes herself to be the girl standing outside Bill Gee's shop, which the correspondent has marked with a cross!

10. Mill Street on a summer's day before World War 1. On the left can be seen the large shop operated by Amies Ltd. at Number 28, which is now occupied by the jewellers Susan Yorke Ltd.

POST CARD.

LONDON & NORTH WESTERN RAILWAY COMPANY

(26)

(FOR ADDRESS ONLY.)

"Visit North Wales for a charming holiday. Picturesque Scenery, Grand Mountain Views, Waterfalls, Lakes, Popular Seaside Attractions, and Excellent Hotels and Boarding Houses.

Gentlemen who want a really serviceable every-day boot should see our 8/6 "Juno," in Box Calf (No. D652) Laced, as design, also made in Derby pattern, at 8/11 (No. D694). These are specially good value and are stocked in numerous fittings.

Are you of those who have never tried a pair? Do so at once; they will please you.

A good Shoe for Ladies is our "Society" Shoe at 9/3, in Glace Kid, with 39 sizes to select from.

Our own Specialities—"Society" and "Juno." Repairs by experienced workmen. "Society" Polish, 1d., 3d., 4½d.

AMIES LTD., 28, MILL STREET, MACCLESFIELD.

A. E. Bradburn Esq
34 Beech Lane
Macclesfield
Cheshire

11. A very rare advertising card detailing footwear bargains from **Amies Ltd. of Mill Street**. Note the prices of the shoe polish! This card was issued about 1907 by the L and NW Railway Co. and the front publicises the beauties of Aberglaslyn, North Wales.

12. Mill Street, looking down the hill with the entrance to Queen Victoria Street on the left. Dated 1914 the card was sent to a Miss Ada Brassington in Stoke-on-Trent from "Bert and May" and contains the fascinating message; "Dear Ada, This is the street where the barrel of treacle fell off the wagon, so they always call Macclesfield Treacle Town."

13. Mill Street circa 1907 showing various shops. Clearly visible is the famous 'padlock' sign of Brown's, the premises now occupied by MacDonald's.

Mill Street, Macclesfield

W. H. Series. 2062

14. Mill Street well before 1905. Looking uphill one can see Pickford Street on the right and the shop occupied by Jackson's the jewellers for many years.

15. Park Green, a very old part of the town. This view, taken from Park Street about 1903, shows St. Paul's Church in the distance, now the only spire left apart from that of the Cemetery Chapel.

16. Macclesfield High School, which began life on Park Green, admitted both boys and girls, as this pre-1914 photograph shows, until the Girls High School was built in Fence Avenue.

17. The old **Post Office** at the corner of Park Green and Sunderland Street early in the century. The Post Office later moved to Castle Street, which was not constructed until 1905.

18. Park Green well before World War 1. Visible are the Chadwick Free Library and the School of Art which produced many fine artists, including C.J. Tunnicliffe. The wrought iron fountain was removed and melted down to make armaments and munitions during the Second World War.

19. The War Memorial at the time of the Harvest Festival in 1921.

20. The premises of **James Dixon, Black and White Smith and Horseshoer, in Sunderland Street.** Operating from No. 39 in the same street was funeral furnisher Joseph Lowe, the Undertaker who buried Canadian Giant Leo Whitton in 1899, and who had to hire a brewer's dray and horse to transport the deceased's 51 stone weight to the Cemetery!

21. Waters Green, also known as Albert Place. Posted in 1918 this card bears a special postmark urging everyone to buy National War Bonds! The site is little changed today and the old pubs such as the 'Waters Green Tavern', 'Bull and Gate' and 'Old Millstone Inn' are still there.

22. The **Cattle Market** on Waters Green. This real photograph card by Charles Wilkinson of Manchester shows the scene from the railway station. With the recent completion of the Dams Valley Sewer Relief Scheme flooding no longer takes place and Waters Green now fails to live up to its name!

23. J.J. Cookson established the Central Motor Garage and one of the proprietor's vans, bearing an advertisement for Exide Batteries, is pictured here. The reverse of the card advertises the same product and informs us that batteries requiring to be serviced will be collected and delivered free!

24. St. Michael's Parish Church in the distance and the 'Nag's Head Hotel' and 108 Steps in the foreground. On first moving to the area the author's children required father to take them up and down the Steps to confirm that there were, indeed, 108! Now he occasionally walks down them, but never ascends, wisely preferring to make a detour!

25. Buxton Road with Central Station on the right. Also shown is the low bridge where many high sided vehicles have been jammed over the years. The introduction of electronic warning signs to avoid this situation may mean a considerable expense, but is a cheaper alternative than constant repair of the bridge!

26. Mr. and Mrs. A.B. Houghton and family dog outside their shop, opposite the site of what are now the Flats at Victoria Park.

27. Hibel Road, with an omnibus making its way up and Hibel Road Station to be seen on the left.

28. Fish, chips and Macclesfield before 1918!

29. A carnival procession makes its way up Hibel Road to the junction with Jordangate and Beech Lane about 1930. Amongst the interesting floats is a large 'Saucy One' belonging to the Macclesfield Equitable Provident Society, now part of Normid.

30. Jordangate. A very early view on a summer's day with ladies in elegant white dresses. The flag on the left announces Beds, Dinners and Teas whilst the public house across the road offers Bell and Co's celebrated Ale and Porter. The George Hotel had a very undistinguished frontage in those days.

31. The George Hotel with its revamped frontage. Following the reopening of the Hotel or road (or both!) after the alterations the story goes that the Mayor was scheduled to perform the ceremony but, at the last minute, was unable to take part and a local undertaker was pressed into service, complete with borrowed Mayoral chain!

32. The opening of the **Conservative Club and Assembly Rooms, Castle Street**, in 1925. Views of this street, much of which disappeared to make way for the Grosvenor Centre, are very scarce.

33. The Liberal Club, Queen Victoria Street, pictured in June 1908. This card was sent to a lady in New Hall Street, just half a mile away!

34. Macclesfield Sunday School, Roe Street. Originally founded by John Whitaker in 1796, this building was erected in 1813/14 and its centenary was celebrated on May 6th 1896. The premises are now an important part of the exciting Silk Heritage Project.

35. A group of young people, Indian clubs at the ready, all set to perform outside the **Roe Street Sunday School**. In the background can be seen a poster advertising a gospel service.

Silk

The silk industry has been researched in considerable detail by the Silk Heritage staff and I hope that the illustrations in this book will serve to draw attention both to the Silk Museum in the former Roe Street Sunday School and to Paradise Mill. Having spent more than 34 years in the textile trade, including 27 years based in Macclesfield, I have had ample opportunity to observe the fortunes of the industry at close quarters and in the process have acquired a considerable knowledge of silk — fabrics more than yarn, as I spent a number of happy years with A.W. Hewetson Ltd.

Hewetson's were the largest Schiffli Embroidery manufacturers in the U.K., and the second largest in Europe, employing some 1,000 people. They covered many different outlets and also performed a lot of "facon work", or commission embroidery on customer fabrics. The business was founded by the late A.W. Hewetson in 1898, originally in St. George's Street Mill but later moving to Albion Mills, London Road, a former tobacco factory. After Mr. Hewetson's death the company was run by his daughter Mrs. D.M. Brown, and a highlight in the firm's history was the presentation to H.R.H. the Duchess of Kent of a length of embroidered silk on the occasion of her visit to our premises to mark our 60th anniversary.

In those days the thriving company worked with a wide variety of silk fabrics: Antung, Shantung, Twill, Surah, Moire, Dhobi, Habetai, Crepe, Pongee are just a few that come to mind. The number of end uses was incredible, ranging from parachute silk to postcards and cigarette cards. Our embroideries catered for every aspect of the whole life cycle from birth to death! Morning, afternoon and evening wear; lingerie and nightwear; foundation garments; gloves, handbags and shoes, plus 'special' items such as barristers' robes, church vestments and altar frontals, masonic regalia and so on ad infinitum.

I have fond memories of the annual mill trip to places such as Blackpool, Southport, New Brighton — even once to London! Sadly all this, and the Xmas Parties, came to an end when the company was sold to a finance syndicate!

Hewetson's, of course, were the inheritors of a tradition which began with the use of Macclesfield silk in the button trade as a cottage industry in Tudor times. A leading figure in the eighteenth century growth of the craft was Charles Roe, the son of a Derbyshire vicar, who crossed the Pennines and Peak District to set up in the town about 1744 and, after operating copper mines, joined forces with John Brocklehurst to introduce water power for silk throwing. Handloom weaving started in 1756 and, by the mid-nineteenth century, there were no less than 540 silk weavers in Macclesfield operating looms in their own homes.

Having witnessed the skills involved in setting up Jacquard looms, handloom weaving and the preparation of blocks for hand-printing, I am filled with admiration for these craftsmen and the way in which they were able to work to such fine tolerances in those times.

In the old days I understand that youngsters entering the silk trade from school had to attend school and the mill on alternate days until in the following year they were able to work full-time at the mill. All concerned also had to go on to the mills each Saturday morning to clean and oil the machinery. Eventually the oil-soaked wooden floors became the prime reason for so many mills catching fire in recent times.

The very rare set of postcards numbered 36 to 45 inclusive show Brocklehurst's Mill and the various stages of silk throwing and spinning. The ladies at work are almost as well-dressed as the Silk Queens also illustrated in this sequence!

36. Silk throwing: winding raw silk.

37. Silk throwing: cleaning and winding.

38. Silk throwing: doubling, twisting and reeling.

39. Silk spinning: receiving and opening raw material.

40. Silk spinning: boiling or de-gumming.

41. Silk spinning: drawing preparatory for spinning.

42. Silk spinning: drawing preparatory for spinning.

43. Silk spinning: dressed silk spreading.

44. Silk spinning: dressing or combing.

45. Silk spinning: spinning.

46. A van belonging to **J. Sigley and Sons,** Cardboard Box manufacturers of Pickford Street, and one of the many firms supplying ancillary equipment to the local silk industry. The bodywork of this vehicle was constructed by J.H. Jennings and Son Ltd. of Sandbach in the 1920's.

47. An aerial view of the Hurdsfield Mills complex, the premises of **B.W.A. Ltd.**; Brocklehurst - Whiston Amalgamated.

48. The engine room of a **Macclesfield silk mill**, circa 1907.

49. This windmill was constructed by **Charles Roe** and stood in Windmill Street, Macclesfield, until it outlived its usefulness when it was transported stone by stone and re-assembled at Kerridge. It was finally demolished during the Second World War.

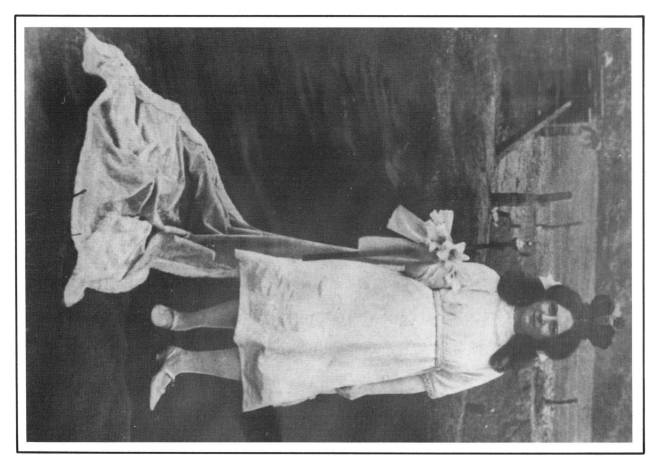

50. Macclesfield's first Rose Queen, **Dorothy Cooper** in 1913.

51. Macclesfield's second Rose Queen, **Miss Florence Bolton.**

52. Miss Constance Richards, the third Rose Queen.

53. The fourth Rose Queen, **Miss Rose Eccles**, doubtless like her predecessors attired in locally produced silk.

BRITAIN'S FIRST SILK QUEEN
Miss Lilian Jervis.

(Madge Dunkerley   Oxford Rd Mill   Macclesfield)

54. Macclesfield's – and Britain's – first Silk Queen, **Miss Lilian Jervis** (later Mrs. Dale) pictured in 1930. She worked at Madge Dunkerley's Oxford Road Mill.

55. A message from the 1932 Silk Queen, **Brenda Goodwin.**

56. Another Queen, **Lilian Handforth** of Langley.

57. Emmie Plant, the 1934 title-holder, in full regalia.

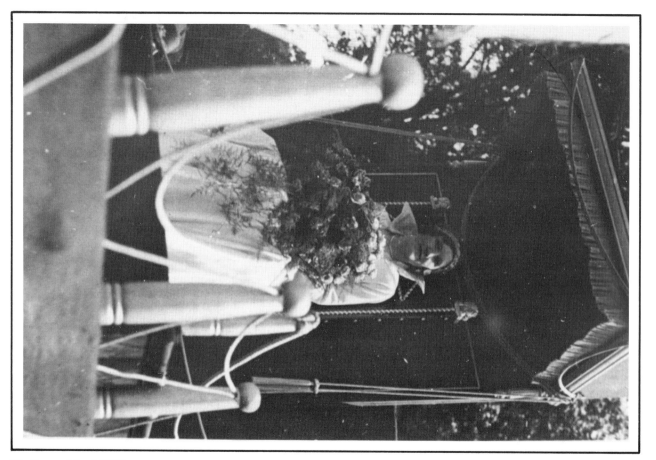

58. Queen **Maud Wilde.**

59. Silk Queen **"Miss Blackburn"**, subsequently to become Mrs. Syd Barlow.

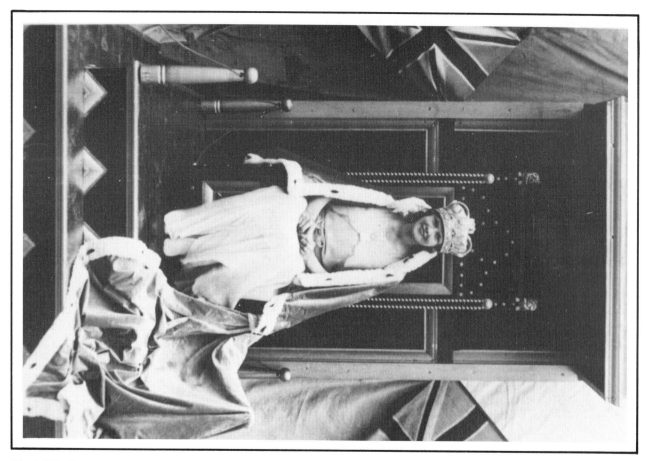

60. A Silk Queen – can anyone identify her?

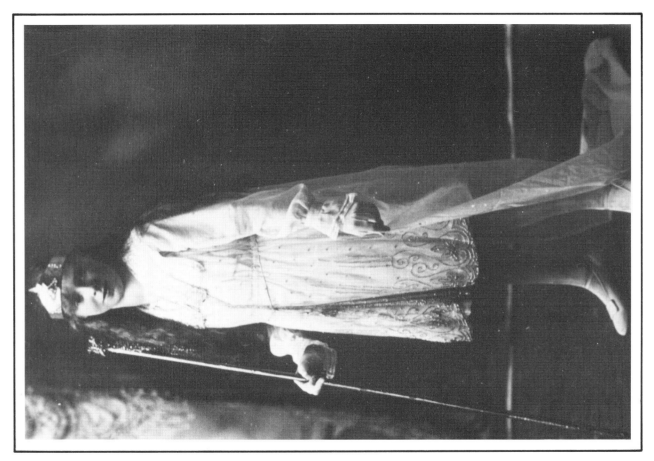

61. Can anyone name this unknown **Macclesfield Silk Queen**?

62. Ross Milk Mills on Mill Lane. Pictured in the 1920's these premises were known to the author as Frost's Mill. Like many others it was badly damaged by fire, but the building has been well restored.

63. Hovis Flour Mill, Union Road, taken from the rear of the premises and showing the Canal which was opened in 1831. Hovis Ltd. were major employers in the town and the Canal was much used by them for the transportation of wheat, flour etc. as well as coal, slate and limestone. The author attended the 150th Anniversary Celebration of the opening of the Canal in 1981 where his friend and colleague, Councillor Reg. Beresford, Mayor of Macclesfield, unveiled a commemorative plaque at the side of Buxton Road Bridge, alongside the original plaque.

64. A **Hovis Carnival Float** in the 1930's. The slogans 'Teas With Hovis' and 'Hovis For All Sports' are well in evidence.

65. Another **Hovis Carnival Float** on the Canal in the 1930's.

66. A barge proceeds along the Canal from Bollington. The Borough Council, in association with the 'Operation Groundwork' scheme, are currently employed in tidying and improving the footpaths along the Canal.

67. The Oak Leaf and Acorn Badge of the **7th Battalion, Cheshire Regiment**, pre-1918.

68. A "thank you" card from the **Vicar and congregation of St. John's Church**, Macclesfield, Xmas 1917.

69. A small group of men from the 'Cheshire', pictured at Oswestry where the Regiment used to camp. Does anyone know their names?

70. Some of the **Cheshire Regiment's injured heroes** from World War 1.

71. Macclesfield's oldest place of worship, **King Edward Street Chapel**, originally built in 1689. Now Unitarian it is still in regular use.

72. The **Parish Church of St. Michael**, badly damaged during the Civil War of 1643 but restored over the years.

73. Christ Church in Great King Street. Built by Charles Roe in 1775, who insisted that the tower be 4 feet higher than that of the Parish Church. Sadly this Church has now closed and is in the hands of the Redundant Churches Commission.

74. St. Alban's R.C. Church pictured early in the century. Designed by a local architect it was intended to have a spire, but this was never constructed. Extensive interior restoration of this Church has, however, taken place.

75. The **United Reform Church** (formerly the Congregational Church), Park Green, at the turn of the century.

St. Paul's Church, Macclesfield.

76. St. Paul's Church, the only one with a spire still functioning in the town.

77. Trinity Chapel, Cumberland Street. The author witnessed the demolition of the spire some years ago and the building is now being well-used as Trinity Elderly Persons Home. On the back is a message dated April 1916 which reads "From the Rev. H. Fytche — We think of you, we pray for you, we thank you."

78. One of the few remaining spires to be seen in Macclesfield, that of the old **Episcopal Chapel** in the Cemetery. This place of worship is no longer in use.

79. St. John's Church circa 1908. It was closed some time ago and a new Church was built on the Weston estate.

80. Hurdsfield Church seen here in the 1920's.

THE MUSEUM, WEST PARK, MACCLESFIELD.

81. West Park Museum, founded in 1898 by the Brocklehurst family. The Museum is sited at the main entrance to West Park, opened in 1854 and one of the oldest public parks in the country.

82. West Park boasts one of the best crown bowling greens in the area.

83. The old **Market Cross**, now adjacent to the Town Hall and Parish Church, used to be located in West Park.

2899.13. Victoria Park
Macclesfield.

84. The bandstand in Victoria Park, off Buxton Road, opened in 1876.

TENNIS COURTS, SOUTH PARK, MACCLESFIELD   95627. Jk

85. South Park's tennis courts, as seen in the Twenties. The Park, which also offered bowls together with pitch and putt, was opened in 1922.

86. Marlborough College (Tytherington Hall) closed and demolished to make way for the Tytherington Estate.

87. King's School, where the author's two sons were educated, was first founded in 1502. Refounded in 1552, first near the Parish Church, later in King Edward Street and finally at its present site in 1856. The Infirmary can be seen in the background to the left.

88. Macclesfield High School, first operated from Park Green and catering in its early days for both boys and girls.

89. Macclesfield High School: the staff.

90 Some of the senior pupils of what had now become the **Girls High School**, located in Fence Avenue. The author's daughter was educated here!

91. Christ Church School, Great King Street, can be seen on the right in this pre-1910 photograph.

92. The staff and boys of **Christ Church School** early in the 20th century.

93. Crompton Road Church School about 1910.

94. The smartly dressed staff and pupils of a **Macclesfield school** about 1910. But which school and who are the pupils?

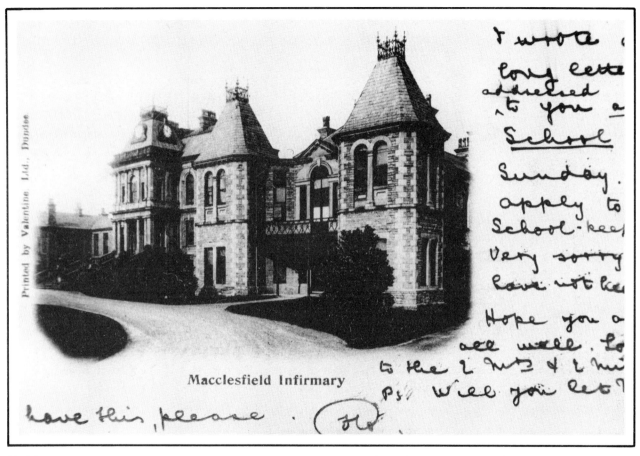

95. Macclesfield Infirmary, the town's main hospital for many years, pictured on a card posted in 1902.

96. Parkside Mental Hospital, illustrated by a postcard dating from about 1910, in the days when the Hospital housed 1,600 patients and was known as the Lunatic Asylum.

97. Collar House, Prestbury, was used as a maternity unit during the Second World War but later catered for the elderly.

98. An Xmas/New Year Greetings Card view of some of the staff at **Macclesfield Hospital.**

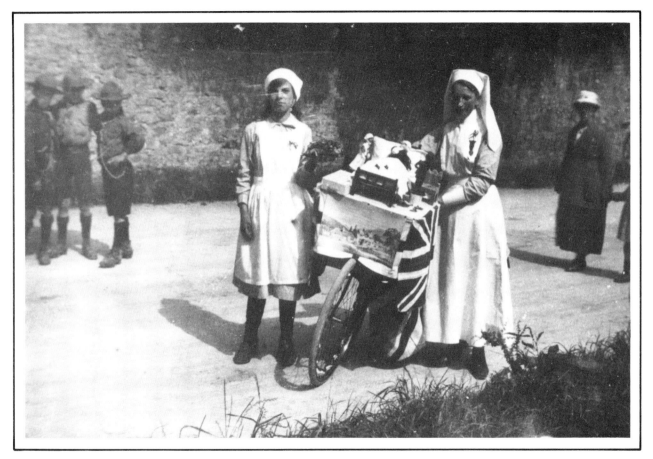

99. Macclesfield nurses with a patriotic mobile display on a bicycle. Note the Boy Scouts standing by in case their assistance is required!

THE ELECTRIC PICTURE PALACE,
Duke St. Macclesfield.

The *POPULAR* and *PREMIER* place of amusement in town
Every Evening at 8. Saturdays 6·30 and 9.
Matinees. Wednesday and Saturday 2·30.

100. The **Electric Picture Palace** in Duke Street. As the caption says 'The popular and premier place of amusement in town; with performances nightly at 8 pm (Saturdays 6.30 pm and 9 pm) and matinees at 2.30 pm every Wednesday and Saturday.

101. W. Gorman's 'Arion' Singers, a Macclesfield group pre-1918.

102. Macclesfield and Congleton Association Boy Scout's camp at Barnswood sometime before 1910.

103. May Day Celebrations in South Park in 1910.

104. A coach trip setting out from Macclesfield for Matlock Bath on May 30th 1927. The speed limit for such motor coaches was 12 m.p.h., although one gathers that it was not always observed!

Just like You! If you once get out of **MACCLESFIELD** You care for **Nowt**

105. A humorous card which indicates the degree of revelry to be expected on a **charabanc outing**!

106. Macclesfield Town Silver Band, 1927-28.

107. Macclesfield Football Club 1907-08. Back row, left to right: Pickford, Yates, Spruce, Robinson, Wareham, Hall, Geo. Milward (Hon. Sec.). Front row, left to right: Alderman T. Savage (President), Woodhouse, Nolan, Case, Howard, Goodwin, W. Fitchett (Trainer).

108. Macclesfield A.F.C. 1926-27. Can anyone identify the players and officials?

BOSLEY SPORTS 1910

109. Bosley Sports 1910 in which many Macclesfield runners competed.

110. Bollington Cricket Club 1906, where many Maxonian men played, including the author (although not so early in the century!). The team members remain to be identified.

111. **A small shop in St. George's Street** before 1918.

112. Pictured before 1920 is this van belonging to **Pott and Thompson,** family grocers and Italian warehousemen.

113. A fine collection of vehicles at **Bollington's Wesleyan Garden Party**.

114. Broken Cross, much changed in recent times. To cope with increases in traffic several old buildings were demolished including that with the clock. The latter was originally mounted at the side of the building but later moved to the front.

115. Buxton Road, looking up the hill and featuring the 'lone stranger', circa 1905.

116. Buxton Road, looking down the hill, about 1905. On the left are the Fence Almshouses.

117. Fence Avenue, which still retains much of the character apparent in this pre-1918 view.

118. Cottage Lane complete with a Hovis horse-drawn van making a delivery.

Cat & Fiddle, near Buxton. The highest licensed house in England. 1690 feet above sea level.

119. The famous **'Cat and Fiddle'** pictured about 1905. Dating back to the time of the French Wars the inn is believed to have been originally named 'Catton Le Fidele' after the Knight responsible for its construction, but the local people had difficulty with the pronunciation. Although usually described as being near Buxton, Derbyshire, it is in fact in the Parish of Wildboarclough, Macclesfield. It is not, however, the "highest licensed house in England", that distinction belongs to the 'Tan Hill Inn' in Yorkshire, which is 1732 feet above sea level.

120. Park Lane, once quiet but now one of Macclesfield's busiest roads. The twelve old terraced houses were known as the Twelve Apostles, although each was not named after an individual saint.

121. High Street at the beginning of the century, now a conservation area.

122. Ryles Park, off Park Lane. Still a residential area it also now houses a large comprehensive school.

123. West Bond Street before 1905.

124. The old **'Flower Pot Inn'** on Congleton Road. Together with the adjoining cottages this was demolished some years ago to be replaced by a large, new 'Flower Pot Inn'.

125. Oxford Road with an interesting view of 'The Beeches'. This card was sent by the occupants to all at 'The Laurels' for Christmas 1906.

126. The junction of **Park Lane and Ivy Lane** in the 1930's. Note the ubiquitous Hovis sign displayed above the Sub Post-Office.

127. Ivy Lane, pre-1920. There are now houses on both sides of this road.

128. Chester Road with a solitary horse passing 'Half Mile House'.

129. Mr. William Bowley, Licensee standing outside the old 'Butchers Arms' at the corner of Chester Road and Prestbury Road sometime in the 1920's.

130. Great King Street, with Christ Church School on the left and the rear of St. Alban's R.C. Church also visible.

131. Ryle Street, near Brunswick Hill, long since vanished from the townscape, but pictured here as it was in 1911.

132. Victoria Road as it was before the First World War.

133. Prestbury Road, with Walker Street on the right, has not changed much from the mid-Twenties apart from the demolition of the old 'Park Tavern' on the top right hand side.

134. Prestbury Manor House prior to 1910.

135. Blue Bell Valley with a few people picking the flowers in the calm and tranquility of a bygone era.

136. Tytherington. A leafy scene now much changed by the building of the Tytherington estate and shops. The reverse of the card, postmarked September 1904, bears the message: "Just met the proprietor of the establishment on the other side, and given me this! I thought I would post it to you!"

137. Capesthorne Hall, home of the Bromley-Davenport family for many years, is located between Macclesfield and Congleton.

Gawsworth
May 26 7904

GAWSWORTH OLD HALL MACCLESFIELD.

138. Gawsworth Old Hall, from a card posted there on May 26th 1904.

139. Adlington Hall, just north of Tytherington.

The people here in Macclesfield are so hospitable, that there is hardly anything they wont do, to ensure one having a good time.

DANE VALLEY, MACCLESFIELD.

TO MACCLESFIELD

140. A romantic card from the **Dane Valley**, circa 1909.

141. Prestbury. A picturesque view of the old village.

142. Bollington, often referred to as 'Happy Valley'.

143. Gawsworth Church, from a postcard sent to A.C. Hague, Officer, R.M.S. "Baltic", (White Star Line), New York, U.S.A. on September 14th, 1906.

144. Disley; the Square mainly unchanged — apart from the traffic to and from Buxton!

145. Alderley Edge; a locally produced street scene before 1918.

GROVE STREET WILMSLOW.

146. Wilmslow; Grove Street is still a busy shopping street today.